Snakes

by Grace Hansen

ABDO
REPTILES
Kids

Visit us at www.abdopublishing.com

Published by Abdo Kids, a division of ABDO, P.O. Box 398166, Minneapolis, Minnesota 55439.

Copyright © 2015 by Abdo Consulting Group, Inc. International copyrights reserved in all countries. No part of this book may be reproduced in any form without written permission from the publisher.

Printed in the United States of America, North Mankato, Minnesota.

032014

092014

 PRINTED ON RECYCLED PAPER

Photo Credits: Getty Images, Shutterstock, Thinkstock

Production Contributors: Teddy Borth, Jennie Forsberg, Grace Hansen

Design Contributors: Dorothy Toth, Renée LaViolette, Laura Rask

Library of Congress Control Number: 2013952311

Cataloging-in-Publication Data

Hansen, Grace.

 Snakes / Grace Hansen.

   p. cm. -- (Reptiles)

ISBN 978-1-62970-061-8 (lib. bdg.)

Includes bibliographical references and index.

1. Snakes--Juvenile literature.   I. Title.

597.96--dc23

2013952311

Table of Contents

Snakes

Snakes are reptiles. All reptiles have **scales** and are **cold-blooded**.

Snakes live in many different places. You can find them in water, **forests**, **deserts**, and **prairies**.

6

Snakes come in many different colors and sizes. Snakes are long and thin. They do not have arms or legs.

9

Every snake has a special
tongue. The tongue is
used to smell.

Food

Snakes eat insects, birds, and small **mammals**. They will also eat other reptiles.

Some snakes kill their **prey** with **venom**. Other snakes squeeze their prey.

Shedding

Snakes shed their skin as they grow. Adult snakes also shed their skin. Especially if it is worn or hurt.

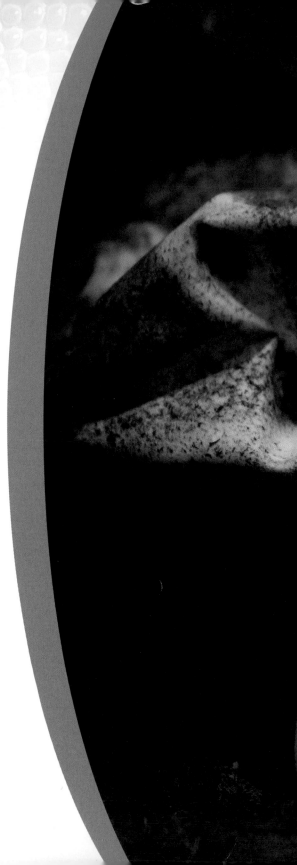

Baby Snakes

Most snakes lay eggs. Some snakes give birth to live young.

Young snakes live on their own after they are born. Snakes usually live for 10 to 25 years.

More Facts

- There are about 3,000 different species of snakes.

- Pythons are one of the longest snakes in the world. They can grow to be over 20 feet (7 m) long!

- Snakes do not have eyelids.

Glossary

cold-blooded – animals whose blood temperature depends on the temperature outside.

desert – a very dry, sandy area with little plant growth.

forest – a large area of land with a lot of trees and other plants.

mammal – a warm-blooded animal that has hair and whose females produce milk to feed their young.

prairie – flat or grassy land.

prey – an animal hunted or killed for food.

scales – flat plates that form the outer covering of reptiles.

venom – a poison made by some animals.

23

Index

abdokids.com

Use this code to log on to abdokids.com and access crafts, games, videos and more!

Abdo Kids Code:
RSK0618